When I look back on my life, you will
have been the greatest infinity to ever sit
with me and love me. I am thankful for
the unexpected encounter who became
the breath in my poetry.

-karnes-

IS INFINITY STILL TEN SECONDS?

POETRY/PROSE

BY: KARNES

1:55PM　　　　9.4.24　　　　Texas

I bit my tongue off as a child to save

myself the agony of being let down,

of being dismissed. It took thirty-eight

years to grow it back. Now, I am free

to speak about the way I have healed.

1:48PM   9.4.24   Texas

My inside voice talks to you often, in whispers, in the
breeze, in the way flowers splash themselves against

the windows to see if you are still who I think about,
to see if you are the name I still use for every word in
my poetry. If I were to tell you all of the things I

believe you to be, you would feel the earth underneath
you break wide open from the crackling of your name

crawling out of my mouth. We probably won't
ever become an embrace, but writing to you
makes you feel close enough for me to
believe in the thought coming true.

5:54PM   9.3.24   Texas

I am between the grasp and open hand, a ray of light
stuck on the other side of dusk. If you are to ever
envy anything, envy the free. If you are ever going

to go after anything in this life, may it be everything
you were told you could not have based on the way
the world had treated others. Lucky for you, you are
not them, and that is exactly why you will succeed

where they failed. It is why you will go down
swinging with love, regardless of how many
times it knocks you back down to hell. The best
parts of life are made from the comebacks.

10:40AM   9.3.24   Texas

You are the kind of love that brings the soul back to the body. I believe in the powers of the universe that brings

together two hearts and hope. I believe in the impossible, maybe too much, but I would not still be here if I thought any differently after everything that

tried to kill me, including the old me. You are the gentle rise of morning, checking on the living to make sure they woke up with enough shine to shelter in.

2:52PM   9.2.24   Texas

Your happiness changes summer into autumn, a
fullness only reserved for certain souls made from
mahogany and rusted sunsets. I wrote about you again

today, but I cannot show you, because I am not here to
interfere with your healing and becoming. I am not here
to sway you one way or another, because once someone

chooses to leave, it is up to them if they choose to
return. Free will is a powerful display of humanity
and love once you understand the value of
the goodbye it sends you.

1:30PM   9.3.24   Texas

You are not someone's project. Never allow
someone to view you as such. The way you
love may never be found in someone else,
but if the effort is there, love them more for
trying. Love them anyway, because one time
in their lives, they were made to feel as if they
were nothing but another excuse to use as to
why things did not work out, when they were
the only ones giving a damn about the ending.

10:57AM   9.1.24   Texas

If you need to heal, take your time. If you need to love yourself more, take your time. September is the month of patience, of summoning courage to find the answers to the questions you have been too afraid to ask. Your shine will survive. Your burdens will come undone once you allow yourself the freedom to choose something you finally believe in and not what someone else is pushing you to do. Create the movement, then lean into each breath that comes from it. Do not go timidly into the fire. Burn with it. Sit with it. Learn why the colors change as they do once the properties of it become something unhinged, untamed, and unwilling to follow the path of the weak.

11:24AM   8.31.24   Texas

I hope perfect never find me. Give me raw. Give me
vulnerable. Give me emotion. Give me what you are
afraid to tell anyone else. I do not want to lose you

because you are frightened of losing yourself to what
you cannot control. I do not want to lose you because
you cannot verbally tell me everything you either have

to paint or hide away in some locked away journal only
your eyes can read. Tell me whatever ache you live
with, so I can at least help you when you feel your
chest tightening do to the stress and fear that
overcomes you in the times of feeling alone.

2:23PM   8.30.24   Texas

I awake at odds with myself. My dreams tell me one
thing and my life shows me something else. Which
wolf do I feed today? Whose heart is going to break
today? How do I move on from you this time?

How many words will it take to write all of this away?
I have a feeling it will be well over a lifetime's worth
once I am finally done writing these books based on
something I used to have and know as love and who

once loved me just as much as the words reflected
it to be in a fullness that could capsize any
human being already mad enough to
believe everything golden always stays
the same shade of sunrise when morning calls.

8:58PM   8.11.24   Texas

She's been in the shadows before, working on her
inner-self. Once the moon leans in, you must listen
and move as she does. We are all searching for more

light to enlighten the way we think and feel throughout
this chaotic trip back home. She has seen better days,
but they have not been around as much as of late.

You can tell when she is having a good day.
The flickering of sin appears in the corner of
her smile, and that is when you know she has
the world right where she needs it. She will never
apologize for being how the world made her.

7:06PM   8.11.24   Texas

Her love is found in the fall, beneath the
crunching of fallen leaves and crisp air flowing
through her hair. She's the ember of the last
fire, of the last dying star, waiting on the spark.
She's the last of the ones who tell you what you
do not want to hear because she knows what
matters most in this world is the goddamn
honest truth. As much as it may hurt you,
it will save your soul in the end.

5:43PM   8.11.24   Texas

You will never catch her without the dreams
she has chased since she was a little one,
because once you find your purpose,
everything else tends to hold you down.
We search for something more in this life
than having someone hold our hand at the
end of the breath. We search for a meaning
that has been undefined since our parents
gave us a name and raised us until they had
to let us go for the world to eat away what
we could never kill off ourselves.

4:23PM   8.11.24   Texas

She was born to be the golden moon. Someone once tried to clip her wings, but forgot what happens to those who wish to do evil things to someone who cut out the tongue of the devil. She is not afraid to hand out death masks to anyone looking to cause her pain in any capacity. There have been those who have tried, but will remain nameless and faceless for only the dead to worry about. Do not let the fear of being alone drive you away from you're the solitude your soul needs.

2:23PM   8.10.24   Texas

Make sure they never forget the scars you wear
were earned by your brazenness, and not by
running into yourself. Everyone thinks they
know someone based off of what their eyes
look like during the night when all that is
around is the moon and what haunts us.
They forget there is more to a human than
the dead we carry on the inside, the love
we never need to speak out loud, and the
secrets that look like tears running down
cheeks made from hands that only knew pain.

1:46PM   8.10.24   Texas

Even in the movements, it has always been
my way of getting as close to you without
disturbing your progress, your healing,
your funeral for your grief. I know this year
has been nothing more than handing out
flowers to those you once loved and knew,
but there is more to it all. I hope closure finds
you each time you are able to visit your father's
grave and not only in the moments that make
you feel less alone by subjecting yourself to
numbing it all away. I hope you know you
are loved, seen, admired, and needed in
every walk of life that has come to know
you by the way you have survived it all.

7:21AM   8.10.24   Texas

May her flames turn my poetry into the embers
that keep the night company. As long you feel
the desire to love, being hurt is always an
option. It is a choice I have made to not
only feel the ache, but to suffer in this way.
I honestly do not know how else to be when
it comes to being me, when it comes to
writing in this form of loss and hopelessness.
Anything can be inspiration. Even my scars
are a reminder that living will cost you
almost everything unless you wish to play
it safe and come out of this empty handed.

6:54AM　　　　8.10.24　　　　Texas

Her youth showed her how innocence can be
the sharpest sword. Adulthood has taught her
how to keep your edge without drawing blood.
As we venture out beyond the womb of our
existence, there is a life begging for our
attention. I hope you find refuge in its arms.
I hope you find the courage to take back
everything others have stolen away from
you. I hope you never forget what it feels
like to have fucking nothing to your name,
so when the time comes for you to tell
someone who you are, you can tell them,
all the angels no one else wanted or could save.

1:12PM   8.2.24   Texas

What we are trying to do has never been done
before. Many of us have tried, but for the rest,
it may be the first time trying to love yourself
more and hate the hurt less.

You must remember that you are worth the
fight just as much as anyone else. You may
have grown up, never knowing anything but
self-destruction and sabotage, but you are here
now. You made it through everything either
you did to yourself or someone else did.

We are not that version of ourselves anymore.
Drop the sorrow long enough to know this is
the tomorrow you had been waiting for during
those quiet moments of being unsure and
neglected by everyone.

12:28PM   8.1.24   Texas

Knowing you are still here, makes the dirt
easier to move from my eyes and mouth.
It makes anything that reminds me of you,
poetry. It could be the sun separating itself
from its core, and I would still find beauty
in the demolition of body and imagination.
To know someone like you is out there and
not being written about properly, prompts me
to sit here, writing for you in ways the dead
poets before me would crawl from their graves
to read with intent and promising gestures
that I am worthy of having their attention.
That I am worthy of having this
translation of soul and body.

12:20PM 8.1.24 Texas

I have seen moons fold in front of you.
I admire your ability to blend in with the
nature around you. It is almost impossible
to tell the difference between you and the
light breaking through the foliage. It has
always been impossible to tell the difference
between you and the awakening that takes
place when you see your chest rise and fall
for something greater than yourself.

2:22PM   8.26.24   Texas

-GROWING FLOWERS IN THE DARK-

I believe in you, in the bravery you are connected with, and in the nature you are made from. You rest your heart on piles of leaves, on stagnant streams where the water reflects what your dreams have a difficult time describing. You are your own savior, a bountiful and majestic creature that seeks out the edges of everything in order to know how much further out you can go until you are breaking through to your promises that you made yourself a few years back. You sit with the sun and moon, and all of their light, because those are the only things that can hold you and be there for you at the same time. I do not know you, but I know a survivor when I see one. I know what warrior's blood looks like. May you only settle for the magic this world gives you, and nothing less than that.

11:47AM   9.8.24   Texas

There are days no one is there for you, but you
continually show up for yourself because you
have no one to run to. You learned early on
what happens to those who have a safe return
to the place that raised them. Bravery is
not something we are born with. It is only
given to those who run towards the fight,
not knowing what will happen after that,
because all that matters in a split moment is
making sure you do more than what is asked
of you. Once you get through it, everything
you once worried about leaves you, and your
second nature becomes trusting your intuition.

3:13PM   9.6.24   Texas

I will be here, even when everyone else leaves,
even when you need to leave yourself from
time to time, you will find me there. I have
been abandoned too often in my life to ever
give you the immense grudge it left behind.
Growing up being raised by, maybes and I
am sorry, turns you into a different breed
of human. The trust leaves. The bond is
shattered. The love for anything you once
found to be authentic changes form and face.
I will not allow myself to be that for anyone
else who needs me. We may be taught
certain things as kids, but it is our job
to break the habit of breaking those we
love because someone else did it to us.
We all deserve better than that.

12:37PM   9.6.24   Texas

You can find her lost in a book, in her mind,
in a thought she once had as a child when all
she could do was hide from her life. There are
a million places she will go in a single day,
and I hope you are able to find her, hold her,
and assure her that whatever happened to her
youth, you will fight like fucking hell to help
her get it back. This year has been one to forget
for her. Anything she thought would work out,
turned out to be another page in her journal
consisting of her rejection and dejection from
this life and those within it. We all go through
several forms of trauma in any given year.
She just happened to experience a few more
that were unexpected, and those are some
you may never come back from, but she has.
She did, because her heart finally caught
up to the fight this year.

1:30PM   9.5.24   Texas

You were always a comforting breath for me.
A place where holding on means through the
dirt below the grave.

Every part of me will make it back to you the
same way the sun returns all its light to the
moon. You can find me in the crevice,

in the crack of her smile. It seems to be
the last place I exist. When her body
reacts to first light, I feel her again.
I am rolling over to hold her again.

6:28PM   6.12.24   Texas   RM.116

Whenever I travel, it takes at least a day
for me to gather my feelings. My thoughts
are somewhere on the road, a few hours
behind me, and I wait until they catch up
with me. Until then, I am a human for a
few hours. I am somewhere in-between a
reality with her and a dream away from
finding her again. A bond was made,
a pact laid over blood and flame,
a promise to be there until the end.

6:18PM   6.12.24   Texas   RM.116

There's no such thing as loving you more than this.
Anything beyond would be me sacrificing the rest
of my life for someone who never comes around
these days. I do not want to know what that feels
like anymore. I do not want to know what almost
having you feels like. I would rather become an
emptied out version of myself, readying everything
left to embrace another who feels as I do when
it comes to love and all of its tragic teachings.

12.29.22   1:55PM   Texas

I do my best to die a poet's death each day I give
more of myself to the paper than with anyone else.
I am far from where I wish to be with my craft,
but a laugh here and there keeps my sanity from
going over the edge where nothing returns except
the truth we all search for. My hands have held
the sun, moon, and dead stars, all hoping to shine
one last time before the dust becomes us.

My wrinkles have lived a full life. Each one earned
and costing me more than this heart of mine could
ever withstand. I was once a drunk who thought
being numb was a proper way to love thyself by
feeling less than human and more of an act in a
show who shows no remorse. I move with the
wind these days. My body leans in a
directionless plea to be seen for the
good still clinging onto me.

9:34PM   12.20.22   Texas

We had it all except for the part when love tried to save us. I wish I could hold you one more time and tell you it is okay if you decide to leave, if this place on my shoulder and chest is not the kind of safety you meant when you said, "Surround me with an entire country of passion." I go through my day still beating myself up about an outcome that was bound to undo all that we had done. I trust in my happiness now, a refuge of all the abandonment I once felt as an eleven year old child when my mother and father divided me into halves and quarters. I remember lying down with you, knowing home was behind your eyes and underneath your tongue. If forever is nothing more than devouring blue skies and sunshine with the one you love, I do not want it. I was born from the fire, and the fire is all I want. The fire does not burn those who were raised by it. I am okay with what is left of its offerings.

7:41PM   1.14.23   Texas

You have worn the thorns for long enough. You have spilled a lifetime's worth of blood for lies you swore were the whole truth and nothing but the truth. You have filled entire rooms with photos, letters, and other belongings you saved from years of merely existing, trying to stay alive so the next day might hurt less. You hide your hands most of the time to remove your nerves from other people seeing it and judging you based off of the age they think you are because of the break down you had last night. I am sure your mirrors are all a bit distorted and gleaming with words you have screamed into it because of how much life fucked you over yesterday and the decade before that. I can tell by your handwriting how often you jump to conclusions and doubt yourself by the T's you forget to cross and the X's you forget to finish which are spaced a few feet away from the O's. The redness in your eyes are not from tears, but late nights when they could never allow the pain to escape. You are a sandcastle awaiting the sea to knock you over and restart all over again on a different part of the beach where humans are afraid to play with the sand and its waves. Where humans are nothing more than birds hoping someone throws bread their way.

1:42PM   6.22.24   Texas

There is hope everywhere you look.
To the sad eyes you see staring back at
you from the mother of three on her own,
fighting to keep the magic alive in her children.

To the man outside of the store, spending
another twenty dollars on scratch off tickets,
believing the next one will be his big break.

To the lonely existing around lovers holding
hands and having the thing you do not.
There is hope in the hopeful when hoping is
the love we are after. Hope is nothing more
than knowing one day, your scars will be
read instead of judged for how they look.

6.26.24   12:50PM   Texas

-A EULOGY FOR TWO-

Long after I am gone, my words for you will always be found and heard by you. I have whispered poetry to the trees, birds, flowers, and oceans, all begging me to continue on, to add more prose for the love I have placed between dusk and dawn, starlight and moonlight, and every gathering eye that has roamed around me while I was thinking about you. You are and have been the beauty I write about. One could say I have written all that is possible about a woman who left, who is no longer waiting on me, who has someone else to listen to when it comes to describing such gentle movements. I hope you never meet someone as I did, because for the rest of your life, you will spend it in-between a world which nothing else matters but making sure she never forgets her smile and glow, and in a world you will eventually move on and die in later without her. The one thing I have learned is if you love someone, tell them. Tell them until the other side of the moon knows your true intentions.

2:12PM   6.18.24   Texas

-FIRST DATE BLUES-

I went out on a date last night and thought of you. I thought about how we never got to, how we never once sat across from one another, eyes locked and bodies starving for the other. I wish things would have worked out instead of me rehashing old memories to feed my aches and lack of love in my life. I left the date, then came back to the house. There was not much conversation during the meal. How could there be when you are out with someone who you wish was someone else. I told her I was sorry for being as quiet as I was and only looking at her a few times during the entire night. My eyes only know you. They only see you. They only seek you. They only know what they want this life to become, and since I cannot wrap you up in these arms and thoughts, no one should be subjected to your absence and the cause of this being the first date I have had in years. There is a proper way of going about letting go. One I have yet to master. One I probably never will. One that may find me one day when I have the courage to go out again with someone and not think of you at all.

1:16PM 6.8.24 Texas

-EMBERS OF ANOTHER LIFE-

I would have died trying to bring the sun back up for you each and every day my eyes became a fixated mark on your sleeping body. I would have died trying to keep the smile that saved my own life when all I had to love me were the scars I had made on my body when pain seemed to be the only friend of mine. You were all of creation for me, and now, all I am creating are poems for everyone but you to read. Maybe one day, you will understand the loss of a heart and how much life bleeds out of you when you had put so much of it into another. I shake with sadness, anger, and confusion, but at least it is shaking the dust, rocks, and dead leaves away and off of me. If I could tell you one thing to hold onto and remember during your travels, it would be to never start a fire in a lover's heart you do not tend to keep ablaze. At the end of the day, we are all pyromaniacs without pardon for our neglectful tendencies when it comes to throwing gasoline on starving flames who have simply been left to burn out by someone who said they would never let the night take our intensity away. My ashes still tell an indefectible tale. At least there is something left of the poetry to be digested by when the forest goes hungry.

1:44PM   6.7.24   Texas

-ADAPTATION-

I once wrapped my arms around the world, only to forget how to embrace myself. There were times I gave too much when I was getting silence in return. When I was growing up, that is what it was for me, so I thought that is how it was meant to feel. My life had been nothing but quiet yells into a pillow, not wanting anyone to hear or help me. I did not want to project my inability to cope with my anger and broken home. I wish I would have been better about it all and asked for more when I knew I deserved my own world, too. I became an outlet for everyone else's issues and misgivings. I was a helper before I knew how to console the parts of me no one else wanted to know. In the end, it helped me to understand humans better. Some only want you to fill in the spaces, while others need you to replace everything, including how they once viewed love and unconditional reasoning. I will take on whatever role I need to, if it means someone else feels less alone and empty.

8:20PM   7.15.24   Austin

The sun begins to set on this city.
Glass reflecting every memory from
the day. You will never forget your
reason to endure the suffering when you
see the images of everyone else in search
of their own. Ever single human I notice,
reminds me of you in some quiet or
subtle way. I cannot describe it any
other way than you appear out of
nowhere, as if you are somehow
controlling where you are in my life
and when to show up missing me
more than I miss you.

12:21PM   5.12.24   Texas

-ZEPHYR-

If I gave you a part of me, would it help you sleep, smile, live a bit softer? I know the pain you harbor is not self-made, but you beat yourself up about it because you feel as though you caused it. You have been barefoot for half of your life to keep the connection, to stay grounded, to be as free as one can with everything you have been forced to keep and deal with on your own. Asking fro help is not easy. Asking for help is not your prayer. Asking for closure is impossible. The world is entering your favorite time of the year. A sign of new, a destination full of hopeful nights when the sky lights up a bit more for those who enjoy soaking in solitude. You may never need me, but you have me any time your space feels too complex or crowded with more of you than you can take. I will give you tender words of encouragement, affirmation, and any subtle gesture to ensure your wholeness is intact. I will never leave you bereft and afraid of keeping in your breath.

2:39PM   5.9.24   Texas

-WHEN POETRY BECOMES AN EMOTION THAT RUNS OFF OF EVERY PAGE YOU PLACE IT ON-

I could have loved the fire back into your eyes, back into the life you were forced to run from. I have thought about how I would hold you now, how I would not have let you go back then if I knew I would eventually lose you as quickly as I found you. Time presses all of my memories together and creates the northern lights in human form when I speak to the stars about you, when I show the moon all of the writings I can no longer show to you now. You took the worst parts of me and turned them into a poet, into a man who never knew how to tell someone he was hurting until the other people in his life were okay first. I would have loved you until our souls were ready to walk the other one home. I may have lost you, but I still feel your tiny hand clenched around mine when the day pauses and causes me to force myself to add more lines to these pages to remember how to never forget who you are and what love is when it comes to eyes never losing sight of you through the fall, through the darkness, through the hell you survived.

1:58PM   5.4.24   Texas

-A DAY IN THE LIFE OF AN OBESSIVE WONDERER-

I often wonder what you have been through, what sadness made you this way, and all of the leftover emotions you cannot use anymore to describe what is no longer alive. I wonder how far you had to run to get away from the self-harm, the hurt, the days of numbing yourself to forget you had to feel anything at all. I wonder how many scars you hide in order to fit in, to be a good human in this fucked up society that will judge you if you say or do the wrong things according to them. I wonder how many breaks your heart has been through and if you thought about staying in bed all day today to make yourself feel more safe than you would by venturing out into a world you still feel you will never belong to or trust. I wonder if you put the bottle down for good or if you are taking a pause until your organs grant you permission again. I wonder what caused your eyes to reflect a sunset when your agony beams through your smile. I wonder if you will be a runaway your entire life or until coming home feels like a fresh start for you and your thoughts. A human can die several times in this life, but only for things that leave without goodbye. The rest of us stay haunted by trying to replace it all.

1:26PM   **9.13.24**   Texas

Find me over and over again. In this lifetime,
it is only you and I. There is no other face I
will ever recognize. There is no other face that
will ever make my own smile the way yours
once did. There is not other body I could ever
lay with that would keep mine underneath the
covers for as long as yours did. I miss the
slowness we created when the entire world was
passing before us, hurrying along and rushing
the death that awaits us all in the end.

3:06PM   7.22.24   Texas

-HOLDING. EMBRACING. HELLO-

If I laid down on my back, with the rain falling down,

counting the drops, the beats between creation and

impact, would you be there with me? If I did not say a

word the entire time, and allowed the thunder to speak

for me, would you take it as me not being interested in

you or would you understand sometimes we must give

into the emotions and soak in what we cannot express

in a calmly tone? If I asked you to hold my hand and

wait for sunlight, would you?

12:00PM   7.20.24   Texas

-YOU ARE THE ROSE THAT
THE SUN GIVES TO THE MOON-

I love how the sun bends your soul to fit every sliver of

beauty and magic inside of it. It is that bending

which becomes the moon's shape and phase for when

the evening yawns and stretches, readying itself with

pillows and covers to find sweet rest underneath it all.

You are the underlying simplicity within city lights

that guide all strangers of it back to where peace

is nothing more than a brand new day with

something to look forward to.

2:42PM   8.22.24   Texas

-FEAR AND LOVE BOTH LOOK THE SAME
WHEN YOU'VE ONLY KNOWN HOW
TO HIDE YOURSELF-

You should see her now. Her bones are not showing and her
wings are growing. There is a fine line between her smile

and frown. The eyes weigh less than they did the day before.
You can still see the scars and marks where she went after

her thoughts by cutting her body to feel something besides
worthless. She recently stepped out of her wheelchair,

her prison for the last two years. An accident she was a
part of that nearly killed off what was left of the
good in her, or so

that is what she told everyone. She still screams when no
one is around, but that is just the fight finally leaving her

heart and being tied down to this earth where nothing ever
seemed to go her way. But she is standing today, all aligned.

2:39PM   8.12.24   Texas

-A SHELTERING HOMELAND-

Is infinity still ten seconds? I have been feeling you a lot
lately, too much to think about, so I sit here and write it all

down. There is blood in your cheeks again, a smile breaking
through the sun. There is color inside of your eyes again

where the wars have been won. There is blood on your
sleeves from the last time you wiped your lips in-between

defending and taking your rest. I know the silence is your
safe place, a deafening dream of getting there one day.

Someone once tried to cut your feet from our underneath
you. All you did was wrap the moon up in your wings.

11:43AM   9.15.24   Texas

Maybe we do not all deserve the same things, but to be
loved in the end for who we are by someone we may
never see coming is what I hope for.

To be seen, to actually be looked in completely by
someone else is a form of intimacy that gets overlooked.
I hope you find it. I hope you have someone there with
you who makes the days less of a chore and more of a
miracle. I hope you never forget the strength it took for
you to stand back up on your own,

and how it feels to have someone lend you their hand,
knowing it will be the last set of fingerprints belonging
to someone else you will ever have to wear.

11:57AM   9.10.24   Texas

The sun shines against the blue marble sky.
There is grace in the air today. There is
belief in poetry that pain is a lover, but its
memory stains each sheet.

Maybe it will all heal on its own and not
need us to care for it as often as we do,

knowing how much we could accomplish if not
for the weight of its dead body around our
necks and on our shoulders.

12:24PM   9.9.24   Texas

Some days, I feel a bit more on the edge of my
thoughts, but I know how far I have to go to
find myself again. I know the journey will
never stop, nor give us everything we
are in search for.

You must have direction, belief, and a clear heart
when approaching such endings. I have been
told softness over aggression, but it all depends
on the monster that awaits us all in the final
battle to regain our life and take back what it
once thought it could have without mercy.

There is no such thing in my life. Blood will be
spilled to get it back, to get myself back each and
every day I feel the pull underneath the
dark edges of this life.

12:52PM   8.4.24   Texas

She never gave up. That was one thing no one could
ever take away from her. You may have thought you
could overpower her, but you forgot how she melted
hell and had the devil asking for forgiveness.

You forgot how she overcame the abuse and the lack of
empathy shown by those closest to her who knew what
she had gone through, but never helped with.

You forgot the time she almost ended it all, but gave
life a second a chance after the light came back into
her life during the most random of moments of
moons colliding in her favor.

1:35PM   7.22.24   Texas

-NO LESSONS NEEDED-

I hope you never waver in the dreams of becoming
the human you wish to one day be. I hope you know
how much a heart can take should not be how yours
is treated by anyone telling you they love you,
that they want the very best for you.

Your eyes deserve to see beauty in every form,
and not just a magic show performed to tease the
life out of you. I hope you take each day as if
everything within it is for you, because it is.
Stay in constant pursuit of yourself.

12:13PM　　　　　　8.3.24　　　　　　Texas

-ENDURE THE FATE-

There is still hope trying to find its way through the storm to clear the path, to help ease the eyes of destruction. May love be fate's saving grace. May it never stumble or fall short of the line. Where you are is where thousands wish they could be. Never take for granted the breath, the heart beat, the steps you make when getting out of bed to wash your face and see what the mirror sees. Warriors are only made and created through struggle, through defeat, through the absence of anyone being there for you in the end. Slay the dragons. Burn and bury the devils. Make amends with who you are now and who you had to be when being alone was the only option there for you when everyone else had already left you to handle your hardships on your own. Raise your shield. Raise the sun. Raise your eyes. Raise your focus. Each thing we do gives us that much more fuel to ignite and brighten our journey. Never give in when your inner voice tells you that you will never win, because victory is achieved through loving as if you will never have it again.

10:47PM   9.17.24   Texas

I have felt you before this breath, this sigh
of roses, this monumental moment of souls
          joining hands around the moon.

You are the grasp, the clench, the holding
of light, darkness, and the shadows between
them. I feel you tonight, with our bodies laid
     horizontal and hundreds of miles away.

I have always felt you as close the bee to
the flower. You are a part of me, this story,
this incredible rescue of light from shadow.

2:03PM   9.18.24   Texas

I am a self-taught masochist, with an unhinged
behavior for sacrificing the good in me for
anything worth keeping.

My defeats are still ongoing, but I am learning
how my pain was never mine to begin
with after all.

I am learning how we pass down what we
cannot harbor safely by projecting our own
deficiencies upon those who will never be able
to come up for air because of the weight it
has added onto their bones.

I am sorry. Those words were only heard
after the knife went into my back as a child.

12:32PM   7.26.24   Texas

-POETS AND THEIR POETRY-

You are dancing slowly again, while I am taking my time slowly dying instead. You come to me often, but never on your own. I fear my biggest regret is letting myself down with this fever dream and its pernicious tactics of making you feel closer to me than what real life presents in actual time. My honesty is needed when it comes to love after you. I know there won't be, there can't be, there shouldn't be, because the only room left is the one with all of your things. I did this to myself. I have given karma a reason to install fears of never being able to outgrow the love I had for you and give it to someone else. I take full responsibility for this absence of both darkness and light. Once you give another all you had left in the beginning, there is nothing but poetry for them in the end when no one is left, when no one is able to read what you wrote.

9:06PM   9.18.24   Texas

I hope one day you will want to know me as much as I
want to know you. It is not easy allowing yourself to
meet someone new, but I will be here if you feel the
need to ask me if the poetry is about you.

I will be here with more words for you that
other eyes have never seen, and I will tell
you again, these are for you, about you,
meaningless without you.

2:34PM   7.25.24   Texas

-THE ONLY BURDEN THAT EXISTS IS BY NOT BEING YOURSELF AT ALL TIMES-

I know you may feel like the world's greatest burden,
but you must remember not everyone can match or hold
your energy, grief, wounds, and the things you leave for
the night to know. You are the perfect amount of human,
with the exact amount of emotion and glow. What you are
feeling now is nothing more than a voice that made your
walls grow taller and put marksmen all around the towers.
Your breath is needed, warranted, and rightfully placed
inside of this cosmic parade. Your soul is needed. Not only
in your boy, but in the lives of those who need you, too.
Not a lot of people have experienced what you have in the
last few years, much less in a lifetime. Sometimes, we do
not know how to treat to a wound we cannot see, so leaving
seems to be the only remedy others can provide. But your
heart is a precious thing, even if you feel it has turned to
stone, there is hope etched and marked all over it.

3:06PM   7.28.24   Texas

-SUNDAY CONVERSATIONS WITH ME, MYSELF, AND I-

I lost you, but you have never left completely.
Somewhere in this universe, there is a bond we made
that stayed together, the red string that keeps souls tied
to the meeting, forming the connection we have now.
Somewhere in this world, there is a version of us that
stuck it through and made it until ninety-two, dying in
an embrace that kept the sky full and happy with all of
the stars, sun, and our moon. It does not take long for a
memory of you to come back to me. Like a photograph
we never took. Like the first poem I wrote for you. It all
eases its way into my heart with the slightest of thought
of how much missing someone can become your entire
life. I feel as though it is my profession, as much as it is
a gift given to me by you. Because of you, I will never
have to wonder what being unable to write feels like
when the timing is off. The fire never burns out or comes
close to burning down what is and has been yours since
my name came spilling out of your mouth, as if you
would have fucking died if you did not say it
as loud as you did for me to hear it.

2:18PM   9.22.22   STG

I am in this for the rest of my life. I want it all. My pain
and yours. Your highs and my lows. Maybe, you can
blame how I feel on my mother or how I push through
because of my father. You have been every sentence I
have been writing. Every dream I have been dreaming.
You left me some time ago, but ghosts have a funny
way of holding onto the living. I cannot make a move
without thinking of you. I know I am running out time
before you say, I do, to someone who is not me.
After that day passes, I will stop trying and give you
away for good. I can only keep you as a memory for so
long until your voice finally leaves my life. We were
something though, weren't we? Two souls once divided
by time and space, only to meet when not even our bond
could keep us together. I honestly do not know what this
life is without you. Before you, it was all a blur. When we
met, it all became vivid and real again. Brand new eyes
and a heart to go along with my scars. The same ones you
kissed and said you loved. Each day is another flower
placed upon a grave. The one others will ask who is buried
there and why your name is spelled out to read, my moon.
You did not save me. You saved my entire fucking life.
Humans like that have never found me before. I hope
another one never does, because when they leave,
the remembering hurts more than the absence.
My solitude has no room for the silence they
leave behind. It is where I will love you, always.

12:58PM   9.19.24   Texas

I thought about how much I do not have in my
life right now due to loss, death, or just life
telling me, "I will be better without it."

It is still beautiful, even with all of the empty
spaces between my hands and arms.
I am still here.

There is a grand beauty associated with
having nothing but your breath
accompanying you.

There is a defined courage sitting next
to you on the bench, as you people watch
to see what others are hiding better than you.

12:44PM   7.19.24   Texas

-THERE IS NOT A LIFE I WOULD EVER TAKE
IN PLACE OF THE ONE WITH YOU-

I am not normal. I am the morning person you cannot
beat to the light. I am living my life and the past one
before my eyes saw what beauty looked like. I am in
a world that is a stage and everyone has strings tied
to their existence, being pulled, played, and swayed
into believing everything they see is real life instead
of some make believe act spun up by those needing
to create stability once the curtain goes up. If I fall
in love with you, I will never forget you. I will
write you into poetry to keep you alive long after I
am gone so others know what it was I had been doing
all along. To love, is to inherit pain. To love, is to be
orphaned by it and to be beaten by it, as if you were the
stepchild it never wanted. But sometimes, everything is
not as it seems. To have loved you for all of the years
I did, I would do it all over again to remind the old life
before this one found me what it was like to hold
you, taste you, and feel you crawl into my chest
and never needing more than us.

12:32PM   7.19.24   Texas

-I AM BETWEEN A FRIEND AND A LOVER I NEVER WANT TO LET GO OF-

I love you, but that is not what you want to hear, so I will

scream out, I hate you, until a mind can be changed from

hearing what you are used to, to it becoming the last thing

you ever wish to hear again. I could wrap you up forever,

until our bodies are placed beneath the cold and forgotten

earth that once gave us a reason to burn it all down together

in a frenzy and frantic, a loving and absurd kind of way.

I will be here, keeping in everything you do not want

to hear, but I will write it for you to read.

2:32PM   7.9.24   Texas

-A FRIEND WHO NEVER LEAVES-

There is a different kind of light in you. There is a deeper
kind of fight in you. Who you are has always been the
dream of the little girl who would cover her face with
a pillow and scream into it everything she was never
brave enough to say out loud at the time. You walk with
the flowers of a past life, a sign of beauty that exists in
those who have known fire never to burn the soul of a
human who kept going back in to save the lives of those
who thought they could do everything on their own.
You are the trees, full of leaves and birds, all in harmony,
as the sun reaches the branches and wings. You are a
symbol of better days, of happier ways adjusting to grief
and all of its messes made by choosing to love something
more than yourself. You are the crown of shells and
sea-glass, a display of hope where hopelessness once
reigned. As you go, so goes the dreams of anyone hoping
to find something more to believe in. Others will follow
after you, but you are the time-stamp of all creation.

11:45AM   9.22.24   Texas

To the poetry still left within you, I will find it and
give you the life you never thought you were worthy
enough to have. May your soul awaken in this equinox,
leaving behind what your thoughts cannot seem to let
go of. You deserve intentional breaths.

You deserve the monuments decorated in your name.
You deserve to wake up without a heavy mind
turning you over to tell you how much you won't
get done and how you won't make it today.

Self-abandonment is something some of us
pick up along the way, if it isn't handed down
to us by our family tree. If you find yourself
in this space, cut it all down and burn the leaves.
No one deserves the shade it emulates.

11:34AM   9.17.24   Texas

You are the rule maker as to who and what is
allowed in. Your heart has always been a
nest for all morning birds. Under the waves
is where she found her breath.

She is seashells and salt formed by the ocean's
tears. Beauty comes from everywhere.
Oftentimes, it is created by a loss
we never thought we could get over.

2:11PM   8.21.24   Texas

-PAINT MY FACE AND LEAD THE WAY.
ANYWHERE IS BETTER THAN PRETENDING
TO BE HERE-

You smile as if you have never lost anything
before. I wonder where you got your composure,
your fearlessness, your taste for flesh of every
human who made you feel less than normal.

The only broken souls I know are the ones who stopped
loving once their hearts were stolen and replaced by a myth
that it will get better and you had nothing to do with it.

Take me to your circus, where the lions hold the chairs and
the bears walk their masters. Take me on the high-wire and
teach me how to walk with mountains on both shoulders.

Show me how glory is nothing more than keeping your head
on your body instead of rolling away. Show me how
mastering yourself looks like walking away from
anything that does not serve you in the end.

2:11PM   8.27.24   Texas

-BIOPHILIA-

You have had better days, and they will come
back around. Straighten out your smile, spine, mind,
and everything that feels bent and out of place.

I know the wind could knock you down most days,
with your worries taking up your heart space,
but do not let what you cannot control get
the best of what is left of a good life.

Your war is not with yourself. The quicker you realize
that, the more you will be able to take up arms with the
true culprit. The rivers in you will be full of bass and
salmon again, with nature boasting about the growth
of trees, wildlife, and evergreen returning.

1:34PM   11.18.22   The Hill Country

-SPIRITUAL VAGABOND-

I wear church bells around my neck to keep the demons away, to make sure my sins can be heard for all the miles left in front of me. I was never religious. It was a temporary belief someone force-fed me to make sure I did not get into trouble that would later find me. But it did not work. Nothing ever attached itself to my bones except a few hymns I still hum on days when darkness needs a friend to get through its tough times. Whatever I did was never enough for my own good. I often wondered why I could never settle and sit still when it was asked of me. My mind is a curious place without curtains to bury my face into when it becomes clear I was not made to be a stage hand. This year has been one of reflection, missing, healing, and little love to show for any of it. I have found peace within my sleep for the first time in a decade. I still wake up with a fog I cannot articulate correctly, but it feels as if I am wearing all the dreams the next day. A heaviness without weight, without a name to describe its phase. I miss your laugh. The nervous one. The one that made me feel okay to feel it, too, and not be ashamed of it. I miss waking up without regrets as I did as a child, when all I worried about was the adventure I would take that day. My innocence was lost within the forest of right and wrong. A morally divide of humanistic efforts describe who I am today. I will never believe in the things you do, and that is okay.

If we all agreed on everything, we would be one long line of sheep, waiting for the wolves to eat us one by one. Maybe some of us are. Maybe some hide behind others to keep their strength strong. When trepidation trips my tongue, I bite it off to make sure I stay and go where I belong. I wish I could tell you broken hearts heal, that they go back to together like silver linings being in love with December air, but we are not that lucky. My gift is being able to go beyond the hell I have dug to house all my feelings and emotions. It is a beautiful thing to have such blasphemy at your call. A sharp wickedness exists all around me. It is how these church bells I wear define me. I am beyond sin itself and nowhere near a saintly depiction of rightly virtues. I am beyond the grasp of help that reaches itself out for me to bring me back from the ledge of where I find myself most days. I never jump. I am simply there to feel what it would be like to have wings for a day and view the world as the birds do; without thought, cage, or care.

1:11PM　　　　　　8-8-24　　　　　　Texas

-888-

You have been dealing with more than what you often

tell others so they are not burdened by the weight of
emotions that have nowhere else to go. You sit with it all

until you take action, be it through meditation, journaling,
or sitting in newly born light. You have been the one for

others when they have needed shoulders and space to hang
their souls on for them to dry, heal, and grow again.

You are in a new head-space now, a healing era, a new
mantra for your new-self and all that comes with

befriending yourself after every world you had been a
part of collapsed into itself. You are a sacred siren,

a hero with a new responsibility to protect your
wounds from ever reopening.

1:50PM   8.5.24   Texas

-EXTRAMUNDANE-

The first time I saw you, you were in black and white,
then I saw the colors fill in what the shadows were
displaying in full. May this month bring you healing
if you need it, a more balanced shift in the sky where
the moon sits with you a bit longer than usual.

Someone like you has been friends with her since birth.
Your eyes tell me that, so does the way you hold the light
with a gentle hand. You have fought for more than most
will ever know, except for the parts you want others to
truly understand. Your new journey will ask more from
you, but you do not know any other way to give.

A bruised heart can still move beyond the pain,
beyond the sunset and sunrise of a mourning many
have yet to experience. Trust your movements,
because with them, you will find the truth you are
looking for. You are a cosmic creature, a stargazer,
a healer for those whose luck ran dry years prior to
them realizing it had happened.

To the dandelion inside of you, may your blessings
and wishes never go unheard. When you breathe,
the birds sing. They have patterned their flight after you.

2:22PM   7.30.24   Texas

-MENDOCINO-

If you only knew how much I think of you, how much
of my entire self is consumed by you, I am not sure
you would be able to understand why I could never tell
you these things. It is not me being afraid of rejection.

I have experienced over a thousand of those. It is me
walking that line of fire and ice, of bone and soul,
of me being here and you being there. You have walked
on rivers before. You have flown with ravens before.

You have spoken and shared meals with both the devil and
the gods. I am terrified to let this out, to give you the night
in return for my life. These days, there are not many needing
or looking for an extra worry or care to carry around.

There is not much room left in the halls for the dancing
partners, lovers, and framed portraits of what could be if
we gave up the gun for a more cordial duel. Something less
deadly, like your back against the wall and your
hands above your head.

But you are not the one to surrender, so I will walk
on by with my words holstered this time.

12:18PM   7.3.24   Texas

-NOT EVERYONE CAN WRITE A BOOK ABOUT YOU-

I could have told you by now that I want more than a
friendship, but rejection is a sickness I am not cured of,
nor is it anywhere on my wish-list. Maybe you are afraid to
be around my sobriety, my way of life and how I need it to
be. Maybe you are not into me as much as my thoughts are
devouring the way I want you in all of the ways. I second-
guess my first words yo you, which leads me down a path
that is full of colorful catastrophes. I have so much to say
to you, but you do not hear me. My fear is getting the best
of me, and another, no, could lead me further into a place
of solitude that only allows my own body to fit in. It is
not that I want to spend the rest of my life on my own,
but if you give me a choice between you turning away
and me hanging onto what I have left of a heart and soul
still intact, I will choose the latter; a self-induced purgatory.
There is more of my story still being written, so I move
my fingers across the keys, like a child of braille in a
helpless manner, hoping I can come back and add your
name next to mine as the characters who made it in the end.

8:03PM 5.19.24 Texas

I hope you find your way within the feeling of
bravery and forgiveness. There is a fine line
between the courage and rage.

Find and know your limits, but never allow
someone else to limit your ability to love well
beyond the sea and moon.

Trek openly and as wide as a thousand smiles.
Take time to rest your weary May and the ache
due in June. Find your love in everything you
do. Find your why in the questions you
must ask to endure a life of suffering
only the broken could love and adore.

12:54PM   5.3.24   Texas

-WHEN SUMMER FINDS THE EAST COAST-

You have been here before, sweet light. The same place you found salvation is the same day you found your violence. You have had your back up against the stars all of your life. The bright side is the lonely side to those who need more than a conquering force to set aside their issues, their needs, and every flowering tree you once climbed to see what the world looked like above the burning landscape. Your mind is holistic and your Christmas eyes are kind to sparkling ways brought on by the countless images you were forced to runaway from during a youth baptized in summer haze and heat. You are a lover of all things, especially an old book from a library that is only crowded on Saturdays when the company inside is better than than the chaos taking place outside of its doors. Your favorite smell is of an East coast beach and homemade iced tea your grandmother would make during the holidays. You tell everyone you meet how much you are like her, and how much you miss her since her last breath was taken back in 2005. You never thought you belonged to anything in this world until you began finding yourself in every song and poem written by Cohen and Springsteen during your college years at the campus your father first fell in love with your mother. The shifting tides are rolling in now. The levees are capable of preventing the overflow of emotions and feelings brought on by an overreaction to the placement of the moon. You are getting closer to the closure of having enough money saved up to buy the truck your father had picked out for you two years ago before he left thins world. You are the granite and chisel, a story untold with golden fireworks decorating every part of your existence.

11:51AM   4.14.24   Texas

-WHEN GRACE BECOMES LIGHT-

I know you have been hurting, and there is nothing I can do about it. I know you have had your knees to your chest, making sure you keep your breathing steady. I know you have had your hands curled tight around your pillow, gripping onto it as if it is the last thing you own. I know you have had sleepless night after restless morning, juggling work, relationships, art, and making sure you are getting enough of what you give in return. You have never been quiet about anything in your life, except when it comes to sharing how you truly feel when the lights go out and you are left in a blank room with leftover energy you do not know what to do with. You are not damaged as others have told you. You have simply walked your own version of hell, carrying water back and forth between this world and the one you never talk about. You are new light creeping into new eyes that went blind from staring into a dying sun you were once told would never burn you. I love how your grace overtakes the dark in me, the used in me, and things nobody ever fucking wanted or cared to hold safely.

10:36AM   9.28.24   Texas

-FALL IN LOVE WITH YOUR FATE-

You may think it is your fault, all of this darkness following you, all of this tragedy kissing your bones, but it's not. I have been a continent of a human. Each part of my body being ruled by differentiating emotions. Each one ruled by its own wildness, not even I could break through to console and care for. I have been left behind by a countless number of those who once told me they would never leave and love me beyond the days left, myself included. I have slid off into the sea, one parcel of land at a time. Waves inducing me and inducting me into a ring of hell no one had been prepared to survive. I have had everything and nothing at the same time, though they both left me feeling as empty as night without a moon. I know you have been hurt by yourself and those who you believed to be a caretaker of your soul, of all of your ragged belongings you had to fight to keep at your side. I know your eyes turn a shade of red from the tears you did not know you needed to shed. You are a warrior, marked by scars and dried blood. You no longer have to carry every shield and sword by yourself. Your decree is purified dignity, shaped by years of overcoming setbacks that would have broken the backs of every God who said they had a spine to stand on.

You are a child of a cosmos, which gave you precious meaning and a full of breath to believe in once actions become an enemy. Do not lower your head, child. Crowns do not make a human, but yours will never fall. Do not be defeated by feelings you are not made to harbor. Even in your silence, your presence speaks a thousand tongues shaped by a survivor's life. Your light is seen in everything with soul, with hope, with a chance at becoming whole again. You will always be someone feeling the flames and soft rain. There is so much we cannot see when it comes to what we carry. We cannot do anything with it but show respect, honor the way it has made us, and how far it has carried us, too. I have seen what life can turn others into and what they ultimately give to others because of their inability to love themselves. If love had a face, it would be yours, all wrapped around your shimmer. You will always carry a heart that will help anyone before yourself.

11:04AM   10.4.24   Texas

I would rather feel the slightest of touches or a single

shade of orange than walk this place thinking I am

better off not being destroyed by it. There have been

times in my life when I believed going unscathed was

the way to a better life, but at the end of the day,

you must collect your scars just like the warriors before

you who walked this earth, looking for anything to

challenge and eventually overtake.

1:18PM   7.2.24   Texas

-ON DAYS I DO NOT MISS YOU,
WHICH NEVER OCCUR ANYMORE-

I used to love the quiet, until you broke through its silence. Now, the noise wraps around me, just as your body once did when you needed more than my hands to hold it. I once thought if I loved enough, with a force beyond what was given to me when my speech became less of a tool and more of a way to announce everything my soul thought it had lost, that I would have the companionship, the relationship, and the epitome of you take, I give. I take, you give. Unfortunately, giving all you can only hurts worse. Maybe tomorrow, the sun will ache less and give more shine to these bleak pages that refuse to take more of the same words when it comes to missing you for the one thousand eight hundred and twenty-sixth day. When it comes to missing you, I draw your face and replace your sad eyes with mine to feel more happy about missing me on days you do not tell me you do. A life lost from love is another one gained from having something for a brief moment you never thought you would be able to cherish, dearly and wholly.

2:51PM   6.5.24   Texas

-DREAMS WILL NEVER SATISFY ME AS MUCH AS EXPERIENCING YOU-

I still remember how you would hide your face in my chest, as you told me it was the safest place you ever felt. I still remember every outfit you wore when you came to see me, and what you had on underneath. Your tiny hands sculpted the poet you see today. Your kisses remain a part of me, just as your memory does all of these years wrapped into a lifetime. I would have held you above it all, above the fray, above your own worries and doubts that eventually cost me, you. I still remember you on your back, my hands moving all over you, as your eyes stayed closed, as your legs began to quiver and shake the earth beneath us. I knew who I had in you, and it is why I never wanted to give you up, which I have yet to do to this day. I still remember the way your mouth was pressed against my neck, begging me to let go for you, to cum for you, aching for me to join you in the next life we were making. I still remember how the sheets went from ice cold to a thousand flames and how you tasted like lemonade during summer's thirst. You remain everything to me, just as the mind and body of every thought that crosses my ravenous state of conviction for the sex you possess.

1:30PM   6.3.24   Texas

-I WISH FOR PEACE WITHIN MYSELF,
MY WORDS, MY HEART-

I have tried turning you into the moon, into the books
I have written, and every page of a life I thought I
would have had with you by now.

I have tried turning you into poetry, prose, long hand,
short hand, and songs about second chances for
soulmates, for hearts made for something more.

To this day, I cannot make you love me. I cannot turn
your absence into anything more than a solitude lifestyle
to keep myself away from anyone else I may hurt in the
end, because waking up without you does nothing but
make my eyes search for you in those who love me
more than you do today.

I often wondered what hell was like growing up,
even though I found myself being raised by a devil
back then. Today, it is a love to give to someone who
does not want what they once told you they could
not live without.

1:36PM   4.5.24   Texas

-SAVE THE DATE-

Do not bury me just yet, darling. There are words that need
to be spoken of which I cannot take with me when I leave.
There are feelings that belong to me of which you gave
to me that need to be expressed.

I cannot take my wits with me when I have yet to sit with
you to collect what has been forgotten. I love that you pray
for me like my grandmother still does, even though we all
believe in different things, the dark holds all of the keys to
every basement where the roses are buried.

Give life to me, slowly. Chance fate one last time. I still
feel you in the morning time, in the seasons of right and
wrong. If you leave me, please, save the birds for me.
I will make a better home to house their
wings, instead of them being clipped by
someone else's heartbreak.

12:04PM   10.7.24   Texas

I am attracted to a gentle light. To be that
kind in this world we live in today, is the
bravest thing one can be. The attraction is
a human meeting the other side of the moon.
For someone to want to know and love me,
it takes a different shade of gray to meet me
in the middle of my emotional moods.

12:10PM   10.5.24   Texas

Only the broken can see the cracks and
know that is where the gold is hidden.
You will always be able to find the
darkness in someone if it is what you
are looking for, but the pureness within a
soul comes from everything that tried to
break it before it had an opportunity to
know a love that stayed because it was
worth it, because it has always been worth it.

1:13PM   10.8.24   Texas

-JUNG-

I will point to you when they ask me who made all
of the flowers, butterflies, trees, and cherry blossoms.
You never thought you were beautiful, not anything to
look at, so you made it all for others to see when they
feel how you once did. I wish you could see how much
poetry and soul you are. You were the letter that grief
sent to me so I could finally understand it is okay to
move on and love, knowing what happened to me
would never change out eventual meeting. You broke
through hell itself to get me out of my own head
and that is why we remain tied.

8:56AM   10.20.24   Texas

There is always a new way to view a sunrise.
Documenting and observing is how I live my
life. You will be surprised to see the changes that
take place within your life once you begin the
practice of noticing rather than believing details
have no merit on the way your body reacts
to the light we cannot see because of it.

9:05PM   10.19.24   Texas

I hope the day brought you everything you didn't
tell anyone about. I hope the burden does not cost
you the good that is left within your body.
I hope you are able to walk this world knowing
there are more full moons to see and more sunrises
that will each ask something different of you.
Wherever you find yourself right now, stand in
a fullness that no entity could ever take from you.

3:37PM   10.18.24   Texas

You have always been river stones and waterfalls.
A little bit here and there. A little bit gone again.
The day itself taught you well, darling.
It taught you how to fly rather than fall beyond
the understanding of how the lows are needed just
as much as the highs are if we are to reach the
potential crawling out of our eyes and hearts.

11:47AM   10.16.24   Texas

There is no other version of me. Even if there were
a hundred other concepts of me, they would all be
looking for you. They would all eventually find a
way to love you again, just as I did the first time,
just as I still do now. There is no other place my
hands want to rest than on yours. There is nothing
more to me than unwritten poetry for the woman
you are. If love can break us and heal us in the end,
I hope you are the one who loves both of them out
of me, leaving me with a bolder way of going about
being human, of being fractured in all the ways
needed for the sun and moon to find me wrapped
in your body, in your moans, in your closeness.

1:25PM   10.10.24   Texas

In the quiet, hands move the shadows away to find the
hiding light. They are the instruments of a good life,
of a better relationship between the lover and its
muse. I am grateful mine have been able to feel
your warmth, your softness, the way you move
when you have everything you need when it
comes to your desires and sexual aches.

8:53AM   10.21.24   Hill Country

I have not had many days or times when I was able to do this type of sable living. To unplug from life and yourself, and plug into the nature and energy that being outdoors brings you is crucial for the balance we all seek. I no longer seek to find. I find myself where the trees block out my thoughts and I am finally at peace with what I hear and what the morning shows me to be love and closure. If you listen closely, you can hear the child you once were, playing and laughing as if life never got the best of you and your heart never tasted defeat and your tongue never tasted blood.

3:08PM   7.15.24   Hill Country

Love me as if there has never been blood coming
from my mouth and out the corners of my eyes.
If you fight for me, I will kill anything that
harms you. Now, and always. I do not have a
middle ground when to comes to fighting for
you, protecting you, keeping you from the devils
that wish to do harm to your lovely existence.

12:15PM   7.20.24   Texas

-THE LIFE YOU THOUGHT YOU WOULD HAVE
OWES YOU NOTHING TODAY. LOVE ANYWAY-

The sun wakes and breaks me in the same breath. It is
another day without you, another five tallies crossed out
on the wall as a reminder of how long I have been caged
within this dream where everything is you, without you
ever appearing. The ghosts will always find you.
Regardless of how much light you blind yourself with,
it can only protect you for so long until you must go
forward again. This is a life I may have not signed up
for, but it has both of our signatures at the bottom in
blood, as an oath, a promise, a sacredness we did not
plan on experiencing. From here, you will be in the
places, in the songs, in the sleeping, in the drives when
freeing my mind becomes remembering the times you
sat across from me, with begging eyes and body,
needing something more to touch you than the water,
sheets, and your own hands. I may hate this feeling
often, but I know it serves its purpose for writing books
and poetry about a woman who will be the reason why
lonely may know my name, but it will never fucking
hold me as you did; unreservedly, deathly.

2:27PM   10.25.24   Texas

-MY OWN TRUTH-

Do not look to fix me or mend what you deem
to think is broken. If you are to be in my life,
be here as I need you, not as you think I need
you to be. Once you attain a certain amount of
setbacks and losses, you understand the value
of truth, honesty, and transparency. Do not
come near me with hidden agendas or believe
I have space or extra room for you to feel sorry
for yourself, as well as with me. My healing is
mine alone, and I will not sacrifice it for any
kind of beauty except for the nature I find
myself in when I am looking for comfort.

10:27AM   10.26.24   Texas

-OCTOBER SKIES-

She never fails in her beauty. Morning comes
and I whisper to the dying light, "I will take
the sun's place if it means her soul will be
healed." I have never seen home in a pair of
eyes with trees and birds I grew up without as
a child. There were times you thought no one
heard your cries and subtle sounds of agony,
but I did. To know her is to know how the
colors became named and arranged in such
a way that it will always take the place of a
darkened shade of guilt she oftentimes feels
waking you not feeling as if she belongs
anywhere. When you feel it coming on,
my arms were made specifically to fit your
silhouette, shadow, and everything you believe
you cannot say out loud. Safety is nothing more
than knowing where you can pause long
enough to get your breath back.

10:42AM   10.27.24   Texas

-HERE BEFORE-

You have been here before, with the same odds
stacked against you, with the same worries
eating at your mind, but you are better now.
You do not have anything to prove now.
You may have less to show for it, but you
have more love for yourself, for the journey
itself. You know the ups and downs better
than anyone, so lean into what you have
learned over the last few years to guide your
focus where it needs to go. There were times
you never spoke it, but this is where you
wanted to be, and this is where everything
you need, you will find. Some days, it takes
being a mountain to appreciate the stillness
more than the time it took someone else to
climb their own. The weight of it all is what
keeps us from falling back into the nothingness.

1:20PM   10.28.24   Texas

-RESTING HOUR-

Days pass before me, folded hands keeping
grief from running loose again. I wish I never
knew it existed. I wish it never knew who I was
or those I have loved that were taken away by
its unforgiving approach to show none of us
are untouchable and everyone gets a taste of
what can happen on given day. I have recited a
few names in the last few weeks. All of whom
are no longer here to say mine return. I saw
your face in the mirror last night. It still haunts
me that I could not help or save you from
thoughts you never spoke out loud. They tell
me to give it time, be patient, and life will be
somewhat restored. For some, maybe, but for
those who have lost more than a few, even the
wind can hurt on days when you are only
asking for a simple breeze to push out the
dead air you cannot breathe in anymore.

1:04PM   10.28.24   Texas

-IT DOESN'T SOUND THE
SAME AS IT ONCE DID-

If I dedicated my life to you, would that be
enough for you to trust me? If I went to hell
and back as I have before for my own life to
kill and parade the devil around the streets to
show others what being free means, would you
be able to follow me then? I do not know how
else to tell you, show you, and give this love
of mine to you when the silence heard between
your heart and mine feels like it means the
same thing as it did when I grew up only
hearing it whenever an apology followed it.
I am sorry to the trees I have wasted and
sacrificed in your name, in all of this.

2:32PM   4.6.24   Texas

-A CLOUDY DAY IN APRIL-

You have always loved to do your art, play in
the colors, emotions, and feelings of what
used to be a playground for the childhood you
were robbed of. You spend more time these
days locked away with yourself, tending to the
scars, the forgotten parts of you that you once
remembered fondly, with cicadas, waterlilies,
and sweet flag. Time can be a monster if we
allow it more space to wreck havoc and rip
apart who we fought to become and preserve.
I know the nighttime is not your favorite time,
but the light will forever seek you out if you
can rummage through the fear of coming
undone by your own insecurity of being
nothing more than a name attached to a face
covered in waterless tears. I will love you
beyond the panic, the offsetting spark that is
your inability to see how beautiful you are
when the darkness comes begging.

11:58AM   5.31.19   Utah

-THE LAW OF LIFE-

If I never see you again, I know I gave you the
best of me. I gave you the absolute best effort
I could with all things considered. I wish we
could have been more. I wish there was more
to say, more to do together. Time is only kind
to those who decide when to move on and let
go of what is not meant for them anymore.
Life is only kind to those who are kind to
themselves when it is the last thing on the
mind of someone in need of closure. I must
work on both, because I have been beating
myself up, thinking it is and was all my fault.
When in reality, I know who I am and what I
can give to the one I love. If this is the last of
us, I am okay with it. I know my best will be
good enough for someone who actually needs
it all the time. Not just some of the time when
it is convenient for them. I have never known
how it feels to be in halfway with anything.
I will not begin that now.

1:24PM   8.6.24   Texas

-GRAYSCALE-

You are the first break of light, a silent whisper of
triumph during a time in your life when being alone
was never what you wanted. Sometimes, it is the
most beautiful gift that we can find. You are better
understood in black in white, a photograph of wonder
and the early signs of summer's dying plea to remain
alive a bit longer. Ember, is your name. It is the early
morning display of courage shown when feeling as if
you cannot make it another day, turns into a wondrous
lifetime built from heartache and self-love. You may
never give your heart to someone else again, and I
would not blame you. This world does not know how
to handle angels and healing souls the same way it
disposes of the leftover parts of what made us good
in the first place. I do not know you, but I hope one
day I am allowed to enter your space, sit down across
from you, and write about the way your face makes
me believe the shine will come back as soon as you
find a common light to help you see your own in
whatever darkness blankets yours.

2:22PM   10.30.24   Texas

-END OF OCTOBER-

I have been keeping your name on the inside
of my lungs for a few years now. Each breath
is given to you without reciprocation needed,
without anyone else needing to know why you
live there. The essence of each letter begins
near the inception of who you were to me
before you became who you are to me now.
No one will ever be able to reach down there
and take you out. Your roots have formed.
Your flowers have all bloomed. The very
breath of you becomes the dreams I find
myself in, aching to never wake up from.
There is light dancing on the brick wall
outside of my window. I know it is you
surviving and staying alive just for my
eyes to see and feel. I love the beauty you
never talk about when you are its home.

2:04PM   10.29.24   Texas

-OBSERVER, OBSERVING-

You have been keeping to yourself for a
while now. Part of it has to do with you
being unable to trust the outside world with
your inside emotional battle. The other part
is remaining hidden to heal what you do not
want others to see or have to worry about.
It has been a long year, a long life, a longer
day. You will lay your head down soon and
think of a thousand things you have no control
over, while you stress and fret over a life you
know nothing about but swear could be
yours one day. You were made for moments
of closure of which have yet to form before
you, causing you to lose sight of other
moments begging for your attention in front
of you. Do not mistake things not working out
in your favor as punishment. Take advantage
of being human, even if it means watching
happiness collide with someone else's face.

1:52PM   10.31.24   Texas

-NOT ALL HAUNTINGS ARE AS REAL
AS LIVING LIKE THIS-

The leaves have yet to change or fall where I live.
The grass is more brown than the day before and
the humidity makes you forget it is supposed to be
a different season of change. You are still buried in
either room three or four in my mind, with no marker to
tell me, but the sounds help me track you down. I wish
we could all remove the masks, the dead and painted
eyes we see with when it comes to holding onto what
has been gone since the last time we had to pretend
that we were already moving on. You are a memory,
a ghostly entity, a favorite time of the year, a sunrise
in the early hours of November, and the last sunset
of October. My soul carries around items and all
kinds of belongings that no longer help or serve me.
I picked up that habit when I was younger to counteract
growing up with nothing but more emptiness than
anyone around me. Maybe I have been dead since then,
but you were the first to see me and hold me without
going through. If I am human, you are the words.

11:43PM   4.7.24   Texas

-WHO HAVE WE BECOME-

You tell me secrets, but they are not for me to keep.
You are brazen, blissful, and partially unavailable
for me to hold. I know there is more to your story,
the one you say is untold and heavy. You must
know my shoulders have carried death, boulders
the size of falsehoods, and empty humans who swore
they had healed. You are not going to intrude into or
upon my space. Nothing is mine here to begin with,
and nothing will ever be the same since I found my
way through the tunnels of my own escape. The only
thing I have left behind of me, are the blood trails from
my hands where my fingernails were ripped away and
my palms greased by alchemy. This is as close as
you will probably allow me to be, some hidden thing
you play with from time to time to feel less alone and
more of a woman for the world to see you only break
in the evening when your solitude reeks of starvation.
If you can hold my hands, I will hold your face, as we
both love what we were told could not be our embrace.

10:52AM   4.4.24   Texas

-MAY THE REASONS BE MANY-

I hope you never give up your destiny, your ability to
see what is there when others tell you, keep moving.
All of us have broken hearts, shards of lust,
and an unwavering identity that only recognizes
love. Your late nights may bring you more pain
than answers, but the empty promises that were
made to you by the one you trusted will become full
and true one day. I could tell you how well I have
lived, but instead, I will share with you how I needed
to survive to get here. I will tell you how the shine
feels on a sunny day in April, with the only worry
being how much of myself I will give to that day.
There is greater loss than love. There is always a
different side to wake up on. I hope you know how
much you are needed by those who struggle with
almost giving up. I hope your scars are not the only
way of showing someone your bravery. If you do
not believe me, I will show you mine for free.

2:00PM   11.1.24   Texas

-QUERENCIA-

One day, I would like to do nothing but hold
you and hear you tell me everything you hate
about yourself, everything you have kept in
when you were by yourself, as grief came to
you and told you, nothing is forever. I am
sure there have been a few before me who
promised you to do the same thing, but they
left right before your heart exited your mouth.
I would like to do nothing by take in a new day
with you and see how far we could get before
you reeled yourself back in because getting
too far away from your own skin hurts the
bones underneath them. I know you are
not weak or afraid to bleed for what you
believe in, but here I am, with blood
dripping from my mouth, down my chin,
taking on everything that has been meant
for you ever since the firs tie we met. I will
name the devils as we go and kill each one
individually, leaving their blood for a change.

1:32PM   11.1.24   Texas

-WHAT I DO NOT SAY, I TYPE-

Maybe you have never meant something to anyone else
but yourself, and I sincerely appreciate that part about
you. At least you know your value and worth. For the
last several years, I have been held up by the trees
reaching out to gather what was left of me from the
last time I meant anything to someone who told
me they would love me for me. My mind works at
a staggering rate to persuade my heart into thinking
they are on the same page, but it has never been the
case, except for maybe one or two times when being
aligned meant falling further behind any capacity to
think for myself. I have been keeping my eyes on
my own life for around five years now. Within that
time-frame, I have said, I love you, a few times
and only meant it once. On any good day, I can be
the bastard you never want to meet. On any day
resembling hopeful, I can be the greatest headcase
and poet no one has ever heard of. Most days,
the devil would disown me, and I smile fainly.

10:13AM   11.2.24   Texas

-STRANGELY PERFECT-

I take these thoughts and feelings I awake with,
type them out as quickly as I can, because the
hour is short and the day is fleeting when
you are the meaning behind it all. I know
my reasons and objectives for waking up,
taking in the breath as the light forces my
attention towards its appearance and love for
all things living and dead. I give respect to
those no longer here by making sure I spend
each and every second giving all I have to
the love I must get out of me and put and
place it somewhere within the vicinity of
you. I wish you loved me differently than
checking in once or twice a month, but there
was a time I did not know anything about
you, and now, my everything is you.

10:25PM   11.2.24   Texas

-GRACE RECEIVED-

You are getting bolder, brighter, a more aligned human fitting with its soul. I know the tears do not tell the entire story, but they do represent an absence you carry and have carried since you were five years old. Some of your best friends include nature, oceans, and life no one else cares to see. It is why happiness looks like fresh coffee and being surrounded by strangers when being alone gives you everything you need. You want to forget most of your life when being free meant checking on those you loved before they left this earth and made you to deal with its remains. You carry a few roses within your pockets; just the petals, no thorns. On days that feel heavier than your body, you go to the gravestones, place one at each, say what you need, then inhale a grace received.

2:18PM   11.4.24   Texas

-A WOMAN OF WANDER-

You are the only woman I know who could keep a rose
from dying during the winter's most dangerous season
of lonely. You have held your body up this entire time
by moon light and cheap wine, but your true strength
comes from never falling for the wrong thing at the
wrong time. You have several books left untouched
and stacked on your nightstand, knowing you may
never read a single page from them, yet they are
there as a form of protection to steady a wild
imagination and mind. You have no idea what you
are doing, but you go all-in, regardless of the direction
your body find itself during the day. You do not need
love to know what is and what is not worth your time.
You are a naked face and coffee in the morning,
with just enough clothes on to keep the sun guessing.
You are a fullness only the brave could get close
to, and you would rather keep your hands full of
nature and lyrics than with heartache.

1:15PM   11.5.24   Texas

-A MASK FOR A MASK-

There are coins in the fountains again,
a dreamer still raging on with a belief that
poetry could heal the darkness and curse its
light back to health. You do not have to go to
hell to know where others have gone to chase
out what was never meant to win out in the end.
When I sit behind this machine, this perfectly
built truth-teller, this unforgiving altar bringing
all of death's alter egos to the table to eat,
I learn what starvation looks like when you
stare each one down, eye to eye. I could have
never hurt you at all, which is why I allowed
you to do it for me. A masochist is nothing
more than drawing a face on a piece of paper
and forgetting to add the tongue. I have been
arranged by pain and you learned me all
too well in such a short amount of time.

1:24PM   11.5.24   Texas

-ART IS MEDICATION-

You were almost too young to remember what
happiness was like, so you have spent more
than a half of a lifetime trying to add in
whatever you thought it could be by sacrificing
more of yourself for a quick fix. I cannot tell
you where it is found or how many times you
have to die before it is earned, but I can tell
you that pain is riding shotgun the entire time.
You will either get used to its blinding truth
or you will set yourself on fire to blind the
truth within. There is a way to laugh and
allow yourself to feel the love needed in
order to move forward again, but it all begins
with the honesty you cry and write out when
being alone means finally settling down
with patience for a lover instead of finding
another excuse to sleep with.

1:39PM   12.15.22   Texas

-PRIDEFUL & ALIVE-

She may never be able to speak what is on her
mind, but it does not mean she has not tried.
She will never tell you she has had enough,
because a hungry heart never knows how to
act when life is not full enough to sustain her.
We all come from a place we barely speak
about at the end of the day. Being judged
by the one you love is not ideal living in a
world constantly judging who we are.
She has been fighting her whole life to make
sense of where she is now. The only thing
permanent in this world, is the smile we are
given by those who see us, hear us, and
welcome our utter strangeness into their own
lives. You are the crown upon a lion's pride,
a royal red in every sunset. There will come a
time when more of you is needed, but for
now, a full heart is enough.

2:14PM   12.15.22   Texas

-TODAY, TOMORROW, NOW-

In her dreams, she goes back to the little girl who met
herself for the first time. She was not always cautious.
but living becomes exhausting when even those you
trust keep taking without ever running to you when
you ask for help. You know who you are when the
night begs of you to stay. You have always had
trouble sleeping and calming that locomotive mind
of yours. A glass of wine helps, but you are more of
the entire bottle type. There is no judgment for being
that way. Some of us do not dream enough, and it
shows. Small minds tend to be reserved for those who
do the most harm to not only life itself, but those who
do not understand. Full moons bring the best out in
you. Loving too much is the only proof we have
that shows we are capable of living fully. Yours is on
display infinitely, as the sun kneels next to the Gods
who gave their immortality away so you could live on
forever within these pages and in the hearts of those
who will wake up tomorrow with you on their minds.

9:57PM   6.13.23   Texas

-ASTRONOMICAL HARMONY-

You are made from roses and sacrifice, a true delight to any human looking for the brighter side of night. I know you have been sleepwalking since last May. Maybe even a few years before that. Down every hallway, all up in flames, there is more room for you where you once felt safe. It has been a few thousand miles, a few hundred days, and a handful of moments you wished could be saved. It is not easy being the backbone for such a place, for such an assured heaviness to carry every single day, but there is relief coming soon, sweet child. Unwrap yourself from those thoughts you feel as deep as the ocean is blue. Many will never get this far, as far as you. I know your hands have held onto hope's rope all the way down until your feet were able to touch solid ground. You put trust in the journey before, and I know you will again. Open the flowers, and the rain will wash out what you could never wipe away. Every tear has a story left untold for those who do not have the strength to cry anymore. You are the lighthouse for every ship without a sail, and your light will shimmer for all to see how and why you wear the moon so well. Be gentle with who you are. Even mountains forget who they are when others fear the climb. May you always see yourself as you are; infinite, endless, intrepid, starlight.

1:52PM   11.8.24   Texas

-COLOR OF SILENCE-

You do not say much anymore. Not because
you do not want to, but because if you were
to open up and speak anything at all, no one
would believe that much pain could come
from that much beauty and silence. I am
sure you have kept in more things than
anyone will ever have the ability to do,
but there is nothing proud about the
quietness, which is why you remain
plastered to your hands and own space.
You do all you can to live a normal life,
but as we all know, what the fuck is
normal anymore. To watch you move
is to know how the moon was taught
to flow through time and thought. I hope
you find reason to again. I hope you find
a gathering moment to speak without shame.
Move only when you are ready, dear child.

2:01PM   11.8.24   Texas

-WHAT LEAVES, ALWAYS STAYS-

I did not have much to write about today,
then I remembered you once loved me, and all
of these images came back to me. I often forget
just how much of my life was sculpted by your
ability to see through to the other side of me I
hardly ever spoke about with you You granted
me shelter when I already had the stars above
my head. You granted me peace when I already
had this machine to help separate the noise and
voices within my head. You taught me anyone
is deserving of a love they think they aren't
based on the way someone else can hold them
and make everything pause and stop. You are
the soft light in the morning, showing me
tomorrow does come for those full of sorrow
and ache. If I am never able to hold you again,
I know my memory will always have you in
its arms, tightly squeezing, remembering not
to forget, not to let go at any pause felt.

2:33PM   4.15.24   Texas

-A DREAM WRAPPED IN RAPTURE-

I have written your beauty in the flowers again, in the birds resting on your eyelids and collar. I have seen the fields collect all kinds of tales before. The ones you keep secured in a journal your father gave to you when you were seven years old to make sure the promises to yourself would come true one day if you wrote them out enough. I have done all I could to make sure the dawn kept the light fresh and without edges for you. I have typed a lifetime by watching strangers fall in and out of love because they could never decide how much love to give versus how much love they wanted to receive. You are your own defined journey, dear human. Wherever you find yourself, there will be countless artists doing their best to make your soul live on long after the final star falls to your feet, hoping you pick it up and breathe a new cosmos into it for you both to continue existing where darkness cannot touch you. You can be anyone's nightmare, but you were my dream. You were my only wish.

I do not know what time is anymore. I have lost all motion in my fingers, and counting has become as limp as the trees sitting outside of my window, hoping the sun can shine through again with enough rain to quench the thirst of a thousand mouths. I miss you more than I speak about. I talk to your ghost more than to any real human. You aren't dead. You're just missing from my life, which makes me question what it is I am doing if it isn't running towards you. You are married now. You have left all of me wondering why you did all you did if you weren't going to stay away for good. I know my poetry brings you back. It makes you stumble into a writing that may be about you and allows you to feel something you are missing, but not enough for you to leave him for me. Days and months pass before me without hearing from you, but I can still hear the conversations we had years ago, clear as day, as if I am reliving the same old life we once shared all over again. I am not lost. I am navigating my life around an unfilled hole where you put everything I had been without in a tightly secure place for me. I have loved since you. I ruined it because I knew the thought of you would provoke me to write another book about the way your eyes light up when you had something you couldn't wait to tell me. If infinity is still ten seconds, I know how young our souls were when they first met. I know it only comes around once if you are lucky, because anything longer and you are going to outlive everyone else, because this love we still share, immortals could never fathom, nor could have.

www.ingramcontent.com/pod-product-compliance
Lightning Source LLC
Chambersburg PA
CBHW012036140726

47990CB00010B/3257